Behind the Wire

Prisoner of war camps on Wanstead Flats

by
the Wanstead Flats Working Group

Leyton & Leytonstone Historical Society

Behind the Wire : Prisoner of war camps on Wanstead Flats

by the Wanstead Flats Working Group

published in 2013 by

Leyton & Leytonstone Historical Society

Website : www.leytonhistorysociety.org.uk

ISBN 978-0-9553729-9-5

printed by Parchments of Oxford
www.parchmentuk.com

Illustration on the front cover : One of the many Italian prisoners of war captured in Libya who arrived in London on January 2, 1942. One of the prisoners is still wearing his Africa Corps cap, with its large peak as a protection against the hot sun - AP/AP/Press Association Images PA-16839219

Illustration on the rear cover : Wanstead Flats, 7 August 1944 - aerial photo taken by RAF. On the left is the former Model Yacht Pond (now the Jubilee Pond). To the right of the pond can be seen the huts and tents that housed prisoners of war

Prisoner of war camps on Wanstead Flats

During the Second World War the open spaces of Wanstead Flats were an ideal location for military purposes. Between 1939 and 1945 anti-aircraft batteries and barrage balloons were established there and in 1944 the Flats was an important assembly point for the D-Day invasion forces.

For several years during and after the Second World War Wanstead Flats was also home to a large number of prisoners of war (PoWs). Although the war is still in living memory for some, details about the PoWs and their camp, or camps, are now difficult to clarify. It is very likely that Germans and Italians were housed on the Flats during (and after) the war and there may also have been other nationalities, since the German army contained large numbers of non-Germans. The main location for these encampments was the triangular plot of land bounded by Lake House Road, Dames Road and Centre Road, now best known as the sites of the Jubilee Pond and the fairground, but it is possible there were other locations as well. The following has been pieced together from reminiscences, newspaper reports and official papers.

Italian prisoners of war before D-Day

There is widespread evidence that Italian PoWs were based on Wanstead Flats - and in Stratford - earlier in the war. For example, local residents remember Italian PoWs being held on Wanstead Flats briefly after the Commonwealth offensive in North Africa from December 1940 (Operation Compass), which resulted in the surrender of a large number of soldiers from the Italian 10th Army early in 1941. A temporary camp was set up on Wanstead Flats to accommodate some of the 100,000 or so Italian PoWs en route to destinations far from the frontline, including Canada. One local resident remembers "travel by bus over to Wanstead Flats for its latest attraction" in the Spring of 1941:

1

"For us boys it was like going to the zoo to view the animals. Most looked quite happy, laughing and waving at us. They were in their own battledress on the back of which had been sewn a coloured disc. We guessed that was to mark them out if they decided to take a walk from what, in its simplicity, hardly seemed worth calling a prison camp. Within a few weeks they were all gone".[1]

Another recalls watching Italian prisoners making spaghetti on long wooden tables in a camp next to Capel Road. These PoWs were housed in Nissen huts, while other Italian PoWs were housed in tents in Tower Hamlets Road, Forest Gate, which was a bomb site. "For these PoWs we used to collect snails which they could boil up in a tin can and for this we were rewarded with a haircut".[2] Another resident describes going every Sunday to feed the Italian prisoners in the camp on "the pond side" of Lake House Road. Most of the prisoners were "very cheery and talkative and never any trouble," she recalls. "Even as a young child I remember thinking that the chicken wire was very fragile and why didn't they escape?"[3] And until the 1990s a solitary goalpost stood on land to the east of Centre Road which was widely referred to as the "Italian PoWs' goalpost".[4]

There also seems to have been an Italian PoW camp at Whipps Cross Pond and possibly Forest Gate school site at an early stage of the war.[5] A number of eye witnesses recall seeing Italian PoWs in the area with the distinctive coloured patch sewn onto the back of their uniforms.

---

[1] John L. Hayward, *My Early Years – A Life in Wanstead and Woodford 1929-1949* (Brighton, 2010) pp.85-6
[2] Mrs C. Gardner, communication to authors August 2012
[3] Mrs J. Medcalf, letter to the authors, October 2012
[4] See page 14
[5] Newham History website bulletin board

London Borough of Newham

Above : Nissen huts in Queens Road, Upton Park, similar to the ones, possibly built by Italian PoWs, on the West Ham council prefab site on Wanstead Flats near the junction of Latimer Rd E7

Some Italian prisoners may therefore already have been based on the fairground site prior to the D-Day landings in June 1944 and the Germans either replaced them in the aftermath or simply took over a part of the area, leaving many Italians still encamped there. A report in the *Stratford Express* of hostilities breaking out at around this time between "prisoners of different nationalities" in the camps would seem either to bear this out or to point to the presence of other non-German nationalities among the PoWs:

"It was strange to see batches of prisoners out on the road...prisoners of different nationalities have quarrelled and are to be separated; so one lot are making themselves a nice prison where they will not be annoyed by the others. The camp is flood-lit at night...the men indulge in community singing but they seek their couches early and are not a nuisance to residents of the locality. Few of them would choose, probably, to return to the life they were leading when they were captured".[1]

The position of Italian PoWs in the final years of the war was a strange one. The Italians had surrendered in September 1943 so were officially no longer viewed as the enemy. However, it took the best part of a year to resolve exactly what their status should be and because of the logistical difficulties of moving so many it was not until well after the war that all the Italians who wished were repatriated.

The new arrangements, which came into force in August 1944, gave a range of new freedoms to Italians who chose to co-operate with the war effort, including fraternising with the British public, visiting their homes, going to the cinema and writing two 'airgraphs' a month to their families in Italy. Since a large proportion of Italians chose to become 'co-operators', it must be presumed that many memories of PoWs taking part in local activities – such as working in labour battalions and going to church unattended - come from this time.

D-Day and the German prisoner of war camp

The most easily identified prisoner of war camp on the Flats was the one which held some of the hundreds of thousands of German PoWs captured after D-Day. This was one of more than a thousand camps that were dotted around the country. Many local people – most of whom were schoolchildren at the time – vividly remember this exotic intrusion into their lives.

---

[1] Stratford Express 13/10/1944

4

Wanstead Flats, 7 August 1944 – aerial photo taken by RAF. On the left is the former Model Yacht Pond (now the Jubilee Pond). To the right of the pond can be seen the huts and tents that housed prisoners of war. This is a detail from the fuller version, showing the camp and the surrounding area, which is reproduced on the rear cover of this booklet.

At its peak the camp covered much of the land in the triangle between Lake House Road, Centre Road and Dames Road. It is difficult to be as precise about the time period – but it was certainly operating for at least two years between the summers of 1944 and 1946.

Yet next to no official documentation of the camp has ever been found. The mystery is in part explained by the fact that for much if not all that time Wanstead Flats was not a PoW camp in its own right but one of the 'satellite' camps (or 'hostels') linked to the main base camp in the East of London – Camp 30 at Carpenter's Road, Stratford. Stratford, which at its height was home to more than 1,500 German PoWs, spawned at least eight other 'hostel' camps, including Edmonton, Chingford, Waltham Abbey, Woodford Park, Victoria Park and Wanstead Flats.

Above : An aerial view of Carpenters Road pre-1944. It was known as "stinky Stratford" because of the noxious industries like tanneries and paint and varnish works and bone boilers – the prisoners complained about the smell.

But there was also a blackout on any sensitive information during the war – and for much of the time that included the whereabouts and activities of PoW camps. So, for instance, records of the City of London Corporation, the body responsible for Epping Forest (of which Wanstead Flats forms the southernmost part), rarely referred explicitly to the camp. The Epping Forest committee minutes make no mention of its specific location but they do contain occasional indirect references.

For example, the minutes of a meeting in March 1944 say the committee "drove round the Flats via Lake House Road, Capel Road and Aldersbrook Road and viewed further land to be requisitioned by the Military en route".[1] The following month refers to fairground requisition "at short notice" and observes that the Military would pay fairground losses and "restore as was". In May East Ham Council is protesting to the Secretary of State for War against the requisitioning of Wanstead Flats and in October there is the one specific mention of the camps: "The committee drove round the Flats via Lake House Road and viewed the prisoner of war camps and sundry works being carried out on the Flats en route." Early the next year the Superintendent makes a claim of £500 against the War Department "on the basis of loss of rent for the year 1944/45 which claim has been accepted".[2]

There is also only the occasional reference to the camp in the local papers. A report in the *Stratford Express* in April 1944 implied a change of use for the fairground site, noting that an "austerity fair" took place on a bomb site in Windsor Road. "Monday's fair was made even more popular by the fact that for the first time in years there was no fair on Wanstead Flats".[3] In October 1944 the *Stratford Express* reported that Sir James Griggs, the Secretary of

---

[1] Epping Forest Committee Minute Book No.20, Feb.1941-Jan.1945 London Metropolitan Archive COL/CC/EFC/01/20

[2] Epping Forest Committee Minute Book No.21, Feb.1945-Jan.1948 LMA COL/CC/EFC/01/21

[3] Stratford Express 14/10/1944

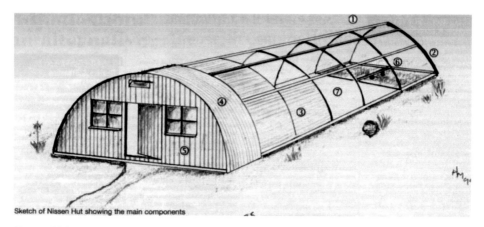

Sketch of Nissen Hut showing the main components

Above : Main components of a Nissen hut

State for War, in reply to a question from a local MP about the protests of local people living near the camp, had assured MPs that the camp at Wanstead Flats was a very temporary arrangement and would be closed before the end of the year.[1] In fact a huge prisoner of war camp existed on Wanstead Flats from at least August 1944, shortly after the D-Day landings, to July or August 1946 when just 10 German prisoners were still in the camp.

During this time Foreign Office representatives from the Political Warfare Executive (PWE) were monitoring the camps at almost monthly intervals to check on conditions but also to ascertain the ideology of those within the camps. One of the aims of the government was to 're-educate' these prisoners with a view to repatriating them once they were judged not to pose any sort of threat. To this end prisoners were divided into three classifications – A, B and C – with C indicating unreconstructed Nazi and A meaning they no longer posed a threat.

It seems from the one specific report on Wanstead Flats, dated July-August 1946, that all the PoWs there were classed as B – that is, grey or in-between. Despite this, it seems to have been decided they could be dispersed or sent

[1] Stratford Express 13/10/1944

8

home because this is the last reference to the camp. The full report reads: "This is a very small hostel with only 10 men. The hostel leader in charge is Oberlagerführer (Camp Commander) Hoppe, B+. A 25-year-old electrician. He is a pleasant type, anti-Nazi but has as yet no constructive political ideas."[1]

The camps

So what were the camps themselves like? In the early years of the war it would seem that most prisoners across the UK were housed in Ministry of War Production (MoWP), Nissen or Laing huts, most of which were 60 feet in length and built in ten 6-foot bays with windows occupying alternate bays. In the South East Nissen huts and Laing huts were the most common construction – but after 1944 the influx of new prisoners was so great that these standards had to be abandoned. From this time on most new prisoner accommodation consisted of bell tents – though a few sites acquired 16-foot span specialised Nissen huts to replace the tents. The guards tended to be housed in more permanent structures.[2]

This seems to be reflected in an aerial photo of Wanstead Flats in August 1944 [see page 5 and the rear cover] which clearly shows a number of hutment-type buildings and tents stretching across much of the 'fairground' triangle of land. Although commonly referred to as Nissen huts, the Wanstead Flats ones were actually a different brand.

The photo also shows tents. There may be anywhere between 150-200 tents visible which strongly suggests that this was where most of the prisoners were held. These may not sound very secure but there was a fence, a guard house and, it seems, the Home Guard was involved in keeping the camp secure.

---

[1] Camp 30, Carpenter's Road, Stratford. Inspectors' reports, 1945-48, FO 939, National Archives, Kew, London

[2] Roger J.C. Thomas, *Prisoner of War Camps 1939-1948* (English Heritage Project Report 2003)

Above : Eden Camp museum Yorkshire, the best-preserved POW camp in the country which is open to visitors. This gives an impression of what a camp of hutments might have looked like.

One local resident remembered a 'tennis court-like' layout of the camp, which accords with the evidence from the aerial photographs.

Many youngsters from the time recall the thrill of visiting these camps and observing their inmates, sometimes taunting the inhabitants, sometimes bartering with them for things like wooden toys. People also used to throw cigarettes and food over the barbed wire for the prisoners. A newspaper report of October 1944 headlined "Prison Camp Sightseers" described crowds "six deep" round the barbed wire watching "jack-booted soldiers" playing football with a rolled-up rag ball, while the prisoners could be heard singing in the evening.[1] Many remember seeing them being marched along Capel Road to carry out war-related tasks such as filling in bomb sites and helping to build the new prefabs that mushroomed on the Flats in the last years of the war.

The *Stratford Express* reported "stories...of girls throwing sweets and cigarettes to the prisoners". This was said to have drawn protests from the British sentries who complained "if you've such things to spare, why don't you give them to us?"[2] There are also reliable eye-witness reports of German

---

[1] Nottingham Evening Post 09/10/1944
[2] Stratford Express 13/10/1944

Above : German prisoners of war inspect displays in the information hut at a PoW camp in Britain.

prisoners cheering on enemy aircraft and shouting "Sieg Heil" as the bombs landed – though on one occasion a rocket only just missed the camp itself.[1]

Prisoners' conditions – preparing for the return home

The German prisoners' lot at this time was, needless to say, not a happy one – though it was probably the case that the alternative of being in war-ravaged Germany at the end of the war was even worse. A local resident remembers his father, who as a home guard was part of the force guarding the PoWs, saying that if the wire was removed and a chalk line drawn round the camp the Germans would prefer to remain where they were well looked after.[2]

---

[1] Cyril Demarne, in W.G. Ramsey (ed.), *Epping Forest Then and Now*, (London 1986)
[2] G. Watson by e-mail 13/05/2010

11

By early 1946, nearly two years after D-Day, and one year after the end of the war in Europe, around 400,000 captured Germans are believed to have been held in PoW camps scattered across Britain. A total of 1,026 camps have been identified although it seems not all of them were actually used. But at least 372 were 'active' and since many of them, like Stratford, had a number of satellite camps, the total number of camps housing prisoners was probably well over 1,000.

Although there are no official records of the treatment of PoWs in the camps on Wanstead Flats, there are detailed files from Camp 30 in Carpenter's Road, Stratford E15, of which the Flats camp was, as we have seen, a satellite. These throw an interesting light on attitudes on both sides towards the end of the war.[1]

PoWs were expected to work at a variety of tasks, mainly devoted to repairing the damage caused by the war, but it seems that many were not paid for this work.

The detailed inspection files of the Stratford camp between 1946 and 1948 reveal that often the main obstacle to the inspectors' re-education work lay not with the prisoners themselves but with their British commanders who perhaps understandably had little sympathy for any efforts to make the Germans' situation more bearable. One early report on the conditions at the Stratford camp just after the war notes:

"Our reception was openly hostile. The commandant said that he thought that screening was utterly useless and a waste of time and also that we were utterly incompetent.

---

[1] Inspectors' Reports, 1945-48, Camp 30, Carpenter's Road, Stratford, (FO 939, NaN-National Archives, Kew, London).

"The interpreter officer Captain Heathcote was obstructive, discourteous and inefficient. He knows no German."

But some of the Germans were just as bad.

"The camp doctor is a most unsatisfactory personality. He is half Danish and only became a German national in 1936. Though ostensibly non-political, he is impregnated with Nazi racial doctrines and a great believer in the superiority of the Nordic race. He believes in euthanasia and sterilisation.

"He is a bad influence in the camp."

And from December of the same year:

"The camp reception was hostile in the extreme.

"Re-education is virtually non-existent in all the hostels. Young PsWs [prisoners of war] were left to rot in their Nazi stew.

"Political re-education is regarded with cynical contempt by the commandant."

And finally in March 1948 the inspector signed off thus:

"This camp has always been a problem and it is with regret that one must record that one has not always had the right kind of co-operation from the proper quarters in the past. Admittedly the stench of the environs may have had much to do with poor attendance at English classes but if only one had had the right sort of people to back up one's own efforts at encouragement then much could have been achieved.

"On the whole it has been a smelly and disappointing camp."

The Germans in the camp were equally uncomplimentary about their treatment, complaining about the conditions as well as lack of information on what was happening in their own country. They tended to blame anything that went wrong on "that abused word democracy", said one inspector. "The most disliked words are 'democracy' and 'propaganda'," he wrote. "An association of ideas has given the latter a wholly objectionable and distorted significance. The former has too close a connection with their captivity." And on one occasion the prisoners even complained that the government's new emergency measures to secure maximum output "smacked of totalitarianism"!

Ironically, the real change in attitude came not so much from the rather ponderous process of 're-education' taking place in the camps (involving film shows and improving literature) but when the prisoners were allowed to fraternise more openly with the local community. PoWs were already being used to help with much-needed war repair work. But as time went on they were also given increasing freedom to attend local council meetings, evening classes, Society of Friends and Peace Pledge Union meetings and each month there were trips for up to 75 to the Royal Albert Hall. A visitors' book

Left : The last of the goal posts erected by Italian prisoners of war on the Flats. Viewed looking north towards Lake House Road, May 1994

from Cann Hall Baptist Church, opened for the church's 60th anniversary celebrations in June 1947, is signed by eight POWs from the '30 PoW Work Camp Stratford'. Meanwhile another PoW was married (presumably to a local girl) at Cann Hall Baptist Church in February 1948.[1]

Some (perhaps including those from the Wanstead Flats camp) were even apparently escorted to Upton Park each fortnight to watch West Ham's home games. As one resident – obviously not a Hammers fan – recalled in an interview:

---

[1] Information from M. Gibbs

Above : Prisoners of war being escorted to Upton Park to watch a West Ham home game.

"They had an enclosure at Upton Park ground for the prisoners of war, they used to march them down there to watch games. Whether they appealed to the Red Cross on the grounds of inhuman treatment or not I don't know (laughs)! I suppose they were glad to get out."[1]

One inspector noted in October 1947:

"Contacts with private citizens are numerous and if, as is stated by many of the German personnel, the new freedom granted to the prisoners is a good thing, and the best form of re-education, the situation is not unsatisfactory."

This shift in attitudes was encapsulated in the inspector's final report in March 1948 when the camp was clearly being wound up. The inspector categorised the remaining prisoners as falling within three different groups – from dislike and distrust (20%) to indifference and benefit of the doubt (35%) and finally like (45%). Of those who were in the middle category he wrote:

"Without liking us ('Who could like the British after they have retained us as slave workers for three years after the end of the war?') their tendency is rather towards the… feeling that 'we're after all not such a bad lot'. 'The ordinary Englishman is more or less a poor devil like us', 'We're fortunate to be in British captivity and not with the Russians', 'Civilians are friendly and help us stock our kitbags' in fact we pass muster although of course – 'England is keeping Germany short of food', 'Grossly underpaid', 'Wrongly screened whereas the SS men all went home' etc etc. Unless this group runs into too heavy a blast of anti-British propaganda when in Germany, the final verdict should be we are at any rate 'erträglich' [tolerable]."

And of those who would return home with essentially good feelings about Britain he suggested some of the most important factors were the freedom

---

[1] Eastside Community Heritage Wanstead Flats Oral History Project, August 2007, interview 22B

they had enjoyed in London together with the friendliness they had encountered from locals. A change of prison commandant had also helped!

His conclusion was reasonably optimistic:

"The men will return balanced in outlook and in the fullest realisation that a Third World War between Britain and Germany is unthinkable...The most important factor in their re-education has been closer civilian contacts and

Left : VJ Day party in Whipps Cross Road, outside the Nissen huts

this in spite of the fact that the majority of the men have been stationed in the heart of the East End of London."

Conclusion

The idea that Wanstead Flats was once home to an international community of prisoners of war from Germany, Italy and possibly other countries can seem like wild fiction these days when all trace of their presence has long since disappeared. Fortunately, as we have shown, there is evidence from a number of sources – including archives, newspapers, aerial photos and equally importantly local residents' memories – to demonstrate without question that prisoner of war camps once existed here.

That evidence builds up a convincing picture not only of where the camps were situated and when they existed but also who populated them and their relationship with local residents. We also get a hint of what camp life must have been like towards the end of the war and in the years afterwards before most were repatriated.

There is nevertheless much about this narrative that remains tantalisingly out of reach. Although we have many local residents' recollections of the time, we have none from prisoners of war themselves. What were their memories of this time? And what happened to those who stayed in this country and perhaps brought up families in the local area? It may be that this monograph helps to tease out some of this information.

The Second World War as experienced by those on the home front was a remarkable and unique time in the history of Britain and of this area. Undoubtedly, the Wanstead Flats prisoner of war camps played an important - and hitherto largely unrecorded - part in that history.

The Leyton and Leytonstone Historical Society's Wanstead Flats working group consists of: Ron Allen, Andrew Cole, Mark Gorman, Alison Rutherford and Peter Williams.

Sources

Archive material on Prisoner of War camps in Britain during World War II is very limited. For the Wanstead Flats camps sources used included Foreign Office papers at the National Archives and the City of London's records at the London Metropolitan Archive. The aerial reconnaissance photograph was obtained from English Heritage's National Monuments Record held at Swindon. A number of local residents contributed their memories, either orally or in writing, which the authors wish to acknowledge with sincere thanks. There are still many gaps in our knowledge about the PoW camps, and we would like to hear from anyone who can add to our understanding.

You can email us at : pows.wanstead@gmail.com

Acknowledgement of sources for the illustrations :

Front cover : by permission of the Press Association reference AP/AP/Press Association Images PA- 16839219

Page 3 : from the website Newhamstory http://www.newhamstory.com/

Page 5 and rear cover : aerial photo taken by RAF, source: NMR/English Heritage Archive, Swindon photo 3309

Page 6 : aerial view of Carpenters Road in Abercrombie's Greater London Plan as reproduced on the website 'Games Monitor'

Page 8 : Wymondham College Remembered http://www.wcremembered.co.uk/nissen2.jpg

Page 10 : Eden Camp Modern History Theme Museum http://www.edencamp.co.uk/

Page 11 : Imperial War Museum © IWM (D 26724)

Page 14 : http://www.wansteadwildlife.org.uk/LOCATION_FILES/WANSTEAD_FLATS/wanstead_flats_photos/wanstead_flats_photos_08_wartime.htm - thanks to Paul Ferris for permission to reproduce

Page 15 : http://www.radiomarconi.com/marconi/monumento/pow/pows.html

Page 17 : http://www.guardian-series.co.uk/localhistory/4461663.Waltham Forest Guardian